S0-BZJ-452

HOW

HISTORY OPENS WINDOWS

The INCAS

JANE SHUTER

Heinemann Library
Chicago, Illinois

Published by Heinemann Library,
an imprint of Reed Educational & Professional Publishing,
Chicago, Illinois
Customer Service 888-454-2279
Visit our website at www.heinemannlibrary.com

Designed by Roslyn Broder
Printed in Hong Kong

06 05 04 03 02
10 9 8 7 6 5 4 3 2 1

Library of Congress Cataloging-in-Publication Data

Shuter, Jane.
The Incas / Jane Shuter.
p. cm. – (History opens windows)
Includes bibliographical references and index.
Summary: Presents an overview of the Incan culture, examining such topics as government, religion, recreation, domestic life, occupations, entertainment, food, shelter, and clothing.
ISBN 1-58810-590-3 (lib. bdg.) ISBN 1-4034-0025-3 (pbk. bdg.)
1. Incas – History – Juvenile literature. 2. Incas – Social life and customs – Juvenile literature. [1. Incas. 2. Indians of South America.]
I. Title. II. Series.
F3429 .S546 2002
985'.01—dc21

2001004027

Acknowledgments

The author and publishers are grateful to the following for permission to reproduce copyright material: p. 6 Neg. no 5068(2), photo by John Bigelow Taylor, courtesy of the Library, American Museum of Natural History; pp. 7, 18 Gianni Dagli Orti/Corbis; p. 9 Art Resource; p. 10 Bridgeman Art Library/ Museo Arqueologia, Lima, Peru; pp. 12, 22 Tony Morrison/South American Pictures; p. 13 Nathan Benn/Corbis; p. 14 Bridgeman Art Library/American Museum of Natural History, New York; pp. 15, 23 Werner Forman/Art Resource; p. 16 © The Pitt Rivers Museum, University of Oxford; p. 17 John Bigelow Taylor/Art Resource; p. 19 Neg. no 5087(3), photo by John Bigelow Taylor, courtesy of the Library, American Museum of Natural History; p. 20 Jim Zuckerman/Corbis; p. 21 Roman Soumar/Corbis; p. 24 The British Museum; p. 25 Neg. no 5094(3), photo by John Bigelow Taylor, courtesy of the Library, American Museum of Natural History; p. 26 Neg. no 5070(2), photo by John Bigelow Taylor, courtesy of the Library, American Museum of Natural History; p. 28 Neg. no 5088(2), photo by John Bigelow Taylor, courtesy of the Library, American Museum of Natural History; p. 30 Charles and Josette Lenars/Corbis

Illustrations: p. 4 Eileen Mueller Neill; pp. 8, 11, 27, 29 James Mitchell
Cover photograph courtesy of Gianni Dagli Orti/Corbis

Every effort has been made to contact copyright holders of any material reproduced in this book. Any omissions will be rectified in subsequent printings if notice is given to the publisher.

Some words are shown in bold, **like this.** You can find out what they mean by looking in the glossary.

Contents

Introduction

Guaca
Tumbez
Cuzco
Pacific Ocean
Talca
Atlantic Ocean

KEY
Capital City
Other Cities
Important Cities
Furthest Towns
Road System
Edges of Four Quarters Area
Collasuyu Area
Antisuyu Area
Cuntisuyu Area
Chinchasuyu Area

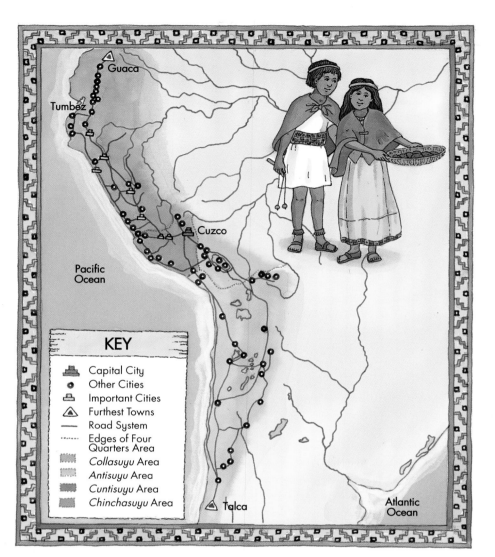

This map shows the Inca empire at its biggest, in about 1520.

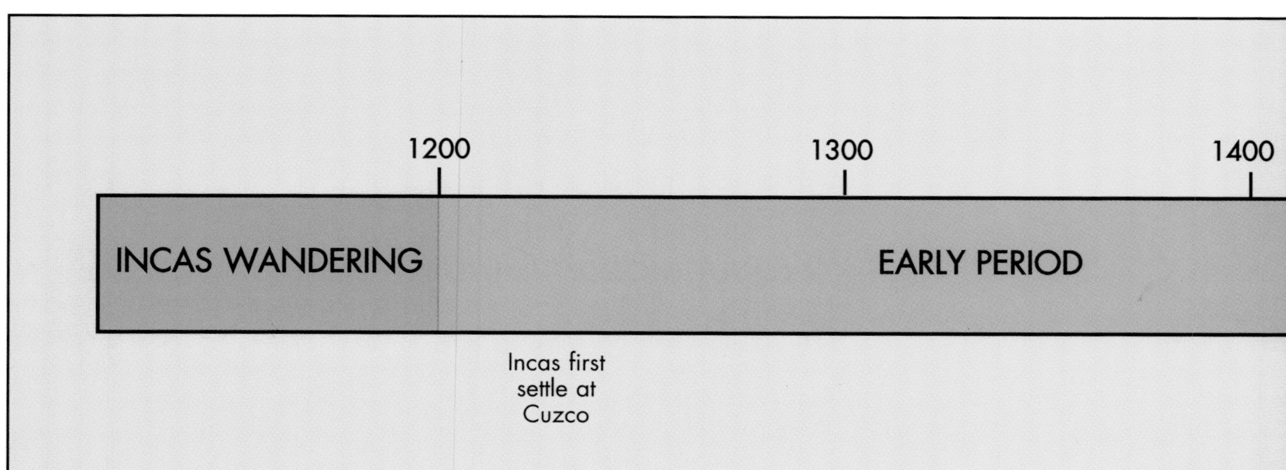

The Incas were a group of wandering people who settled in modern Peru in about 1200. They built a city called Cuzco and farmed the land around it. Sometimes the Incas got along well with nearby groups of people and traded with them. At other times they fought these groups, and sometimes they raided them to take things they needed. This often happened in times when food ran short.

Then, in 1438, Pachacuti became the *Sapa Inca,* or ruler of the Incas. Almost at once he began to build an **empire.** He did this by taking over other lands either by force or by making an agreement with the people who lived there. In less than a hundred years, the empire expanded to cover most of modern Peru and parts of modern Chile, Argentina, and Bolivia.

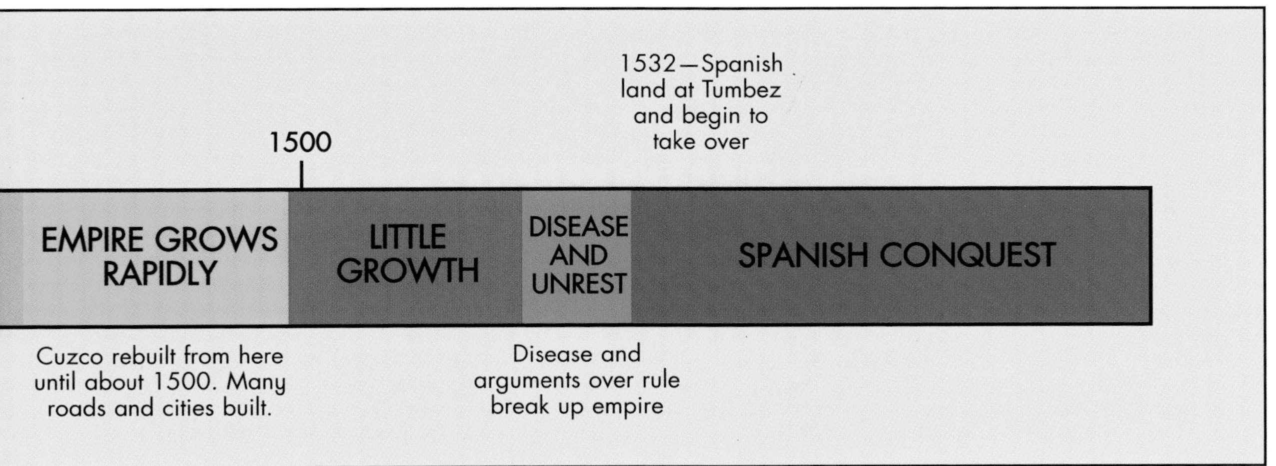
1532—Spanish land at Tumbez and begin to take over
1500
EMPIRE GROWS RAPIDLY
LITTLE GROWTH
DISEASE AND UNREST
SPANISH CONQUEST
Cuzco rebuilt from here until about 1500. Many roads and cities built.
Disease and arguments over rule break up empire

How Were the Incas Ruled?

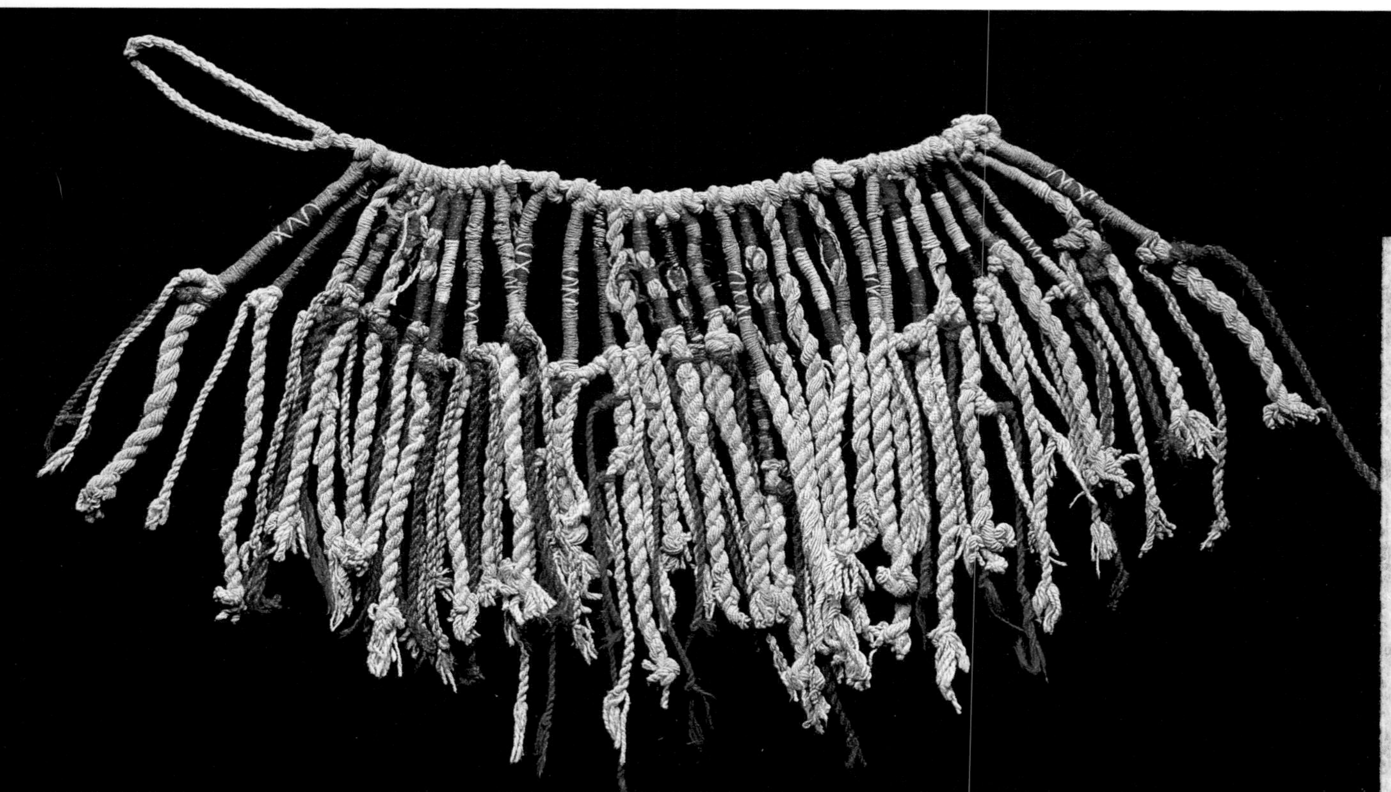

The Incas were ruled by a single person, the *Sapa Inca.* He owned all the land and made all the laws. Unless he died suddenly, each *Sapa Inca* chose who would rule after him. They ruled together for a while so that there was no sudden change.

Each *Sapa Inca* ruled from the city of Cuzco, no matter how big the Inca **empire** grew. Each of them built a new palace in the city and set up a new royal ***ayllu,*** or family. The old royal *ayllu* continued to live in the old palace.

The Incas had no written language. Messages had to passed on by people who had memorized them. Some lists were kept by knotting different colored strings with different kinds of knots. These are called **quipu.**

The *Sapa Inca* owned everything, so he had a duty to take care of everyone. He had to give them enough land to grow their food and enough wool to make their clothes. He had to make sure that there was spare food for years when there was a bad harvest. He had to make laws to keep people safe and make sure they were fairly treated. He also had to make sure that these laws were obeyed. This was a lot to do. So the *Sapa Inca* needed a lot of officials to work for him, to make sure everything got done.

This beautiful golden knife handle would have been made for an important person, probably from the royal family.

Building an Empire

The Inca **empire** grew very quickly after 1438. The Incas would go to the ruler of an area and ask him to join the Inca empire. If he said no, the Inca army went in and took the land by force. The defeated leader had to come and live in Cuzco. He was allowed to live like a **noble,** but he was really a prisoner. This way the Incas could be sure that his people accepted Inca rule.

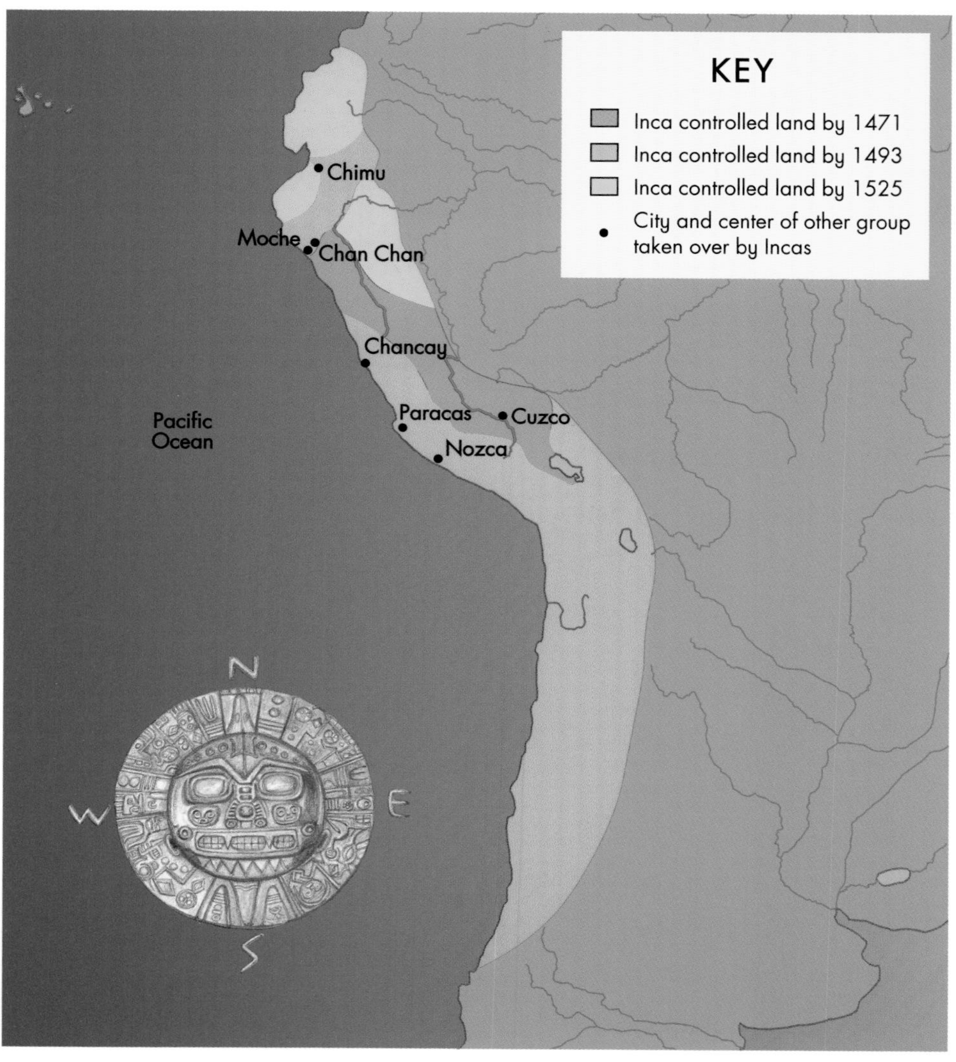

The different colors on this map show how the Inca empire grew.

People in conquered lands brought new skills and styles of crafts to the Inca empire. These beakers are made in the Chimu style.

Once the Incas took over an area, they made the people learn *Quechua,* the Inca language. They made them obey Inca laws and worship the Inca Sun god. If they had taken over by force, they sometimes moved the local people to different parts of the empire, to make **rebellion** less likely. *Mitimaes* moved into the new land. These settlers were loyal to the Incas.

There were good things about Inca rule. They built good roads, as well as cities and public water supplies. They made sure that land was farmed efficiently, and they saw that everyone had food, clothes, and a place to live.

Running an Empire

The Incas called their empire *Tahuantinsuyu.* This means "land of the four quarters." The *Sapa Inca* ruled from Cuzco. He had many officials to carry out his laws, collect his taxes, and make sure all **duty work** was done. An important Inca **noble** ran each of the four quarters of the empire. Each of them had several less important governors to run parts of each quarter. They could be Incas or lords from groups the Incas had taken over.

After the governors came several levels of officials called *curacas.* The most important of these reported to the governor and controlled groups of up to 10,000 households. The least important controlled groups of only ten households.

This pottery head represents a warrior. The Inca army kept control of the ***empire,*** *so warriors were important people.*

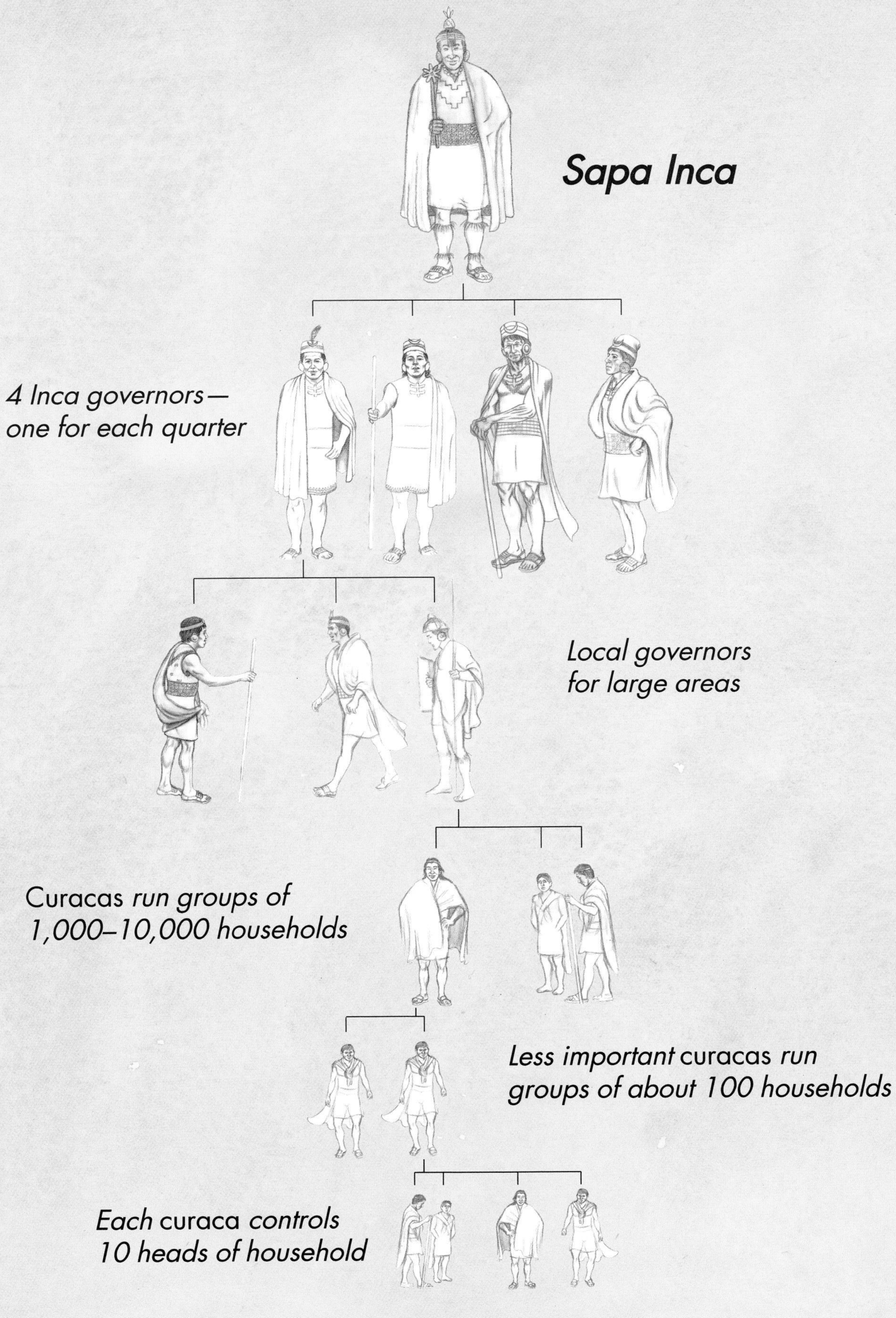

Sapa Inca

4 Inca governors— one for each quarter

Local governors for large areas

Curacas *run groups of 1,000–10,000 households*

Less important curacas *run groups of about 100 households*

Each curaca *controls 10 heads of household*

Roads and Transportation

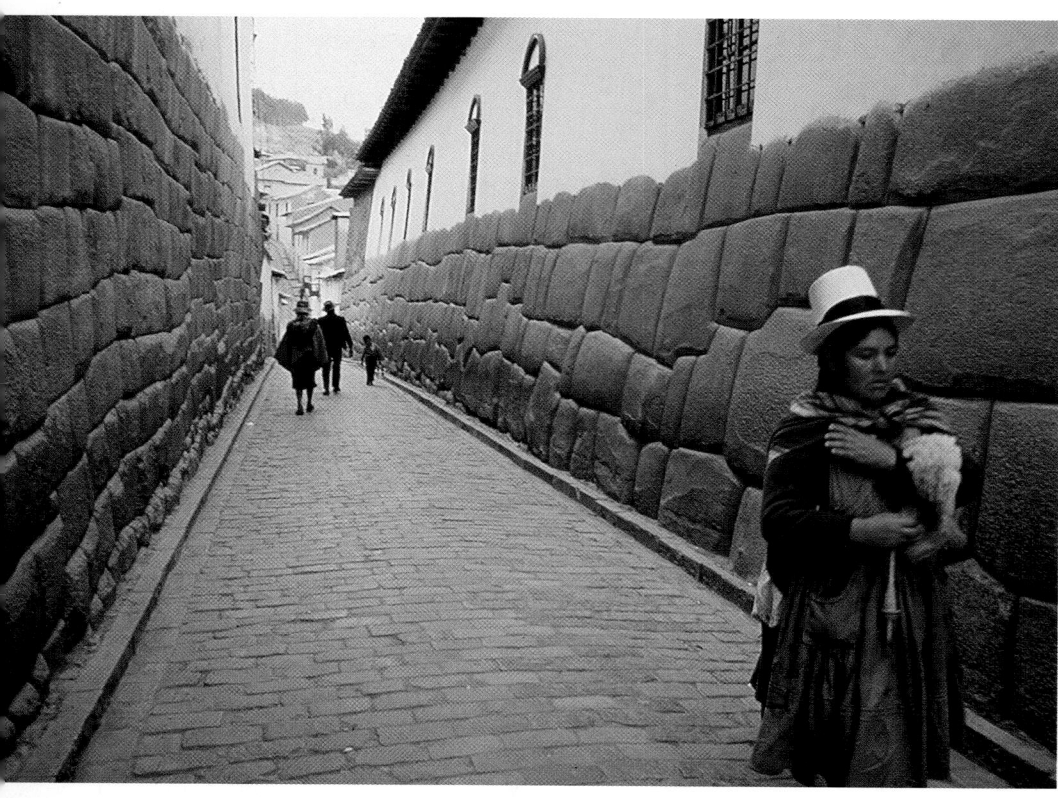

This street in Cuzco, Peru, still has the original Inca road surface and walls.

The Incas did not have wheeled carts or wagons. Instead, people walked or traveled by canoe. Important people were often carried in chairs on poles when they traveled a long distance. Llamas were used to carry loads.

The Incas needed to be able to move around the **empire** easily. They built a road system that covered about 25,000 miles (40,000 kilometers) and linked almost all the main towns. The roads were up to 33 feet (10 meters) wide near big towns. In the mountains they could be as little as 3 feet (1 meter) wide. They had steps, tunnels, and bridges in the mountains.

Not many traders or ordinary people used the Inca roads. They were mostly used to keep the empire running. Government officials used them to move around to carry out inspections. The roads were also used to move the army quickly.

Tambos lined the main roads. These were places for officials to rest or stay in to visit nearby villages. Storehouses were also built near the roads. Messages were sent along the roads using trained runners called *chasquis.* These runners passed on either ***quipu*** or spoken messages. It was said that a message could be sent to someone about 150 miles (240 kilometers) away in just one day.

These ear ornaments show Inca runners. They are shown with wings because the runners were so fast!

Trade and Crafts

Skilled craft workers made these silver models of two alpacas and a woman.

The Incas did not trade much outside the **empire.** Villages tried to grow and make everything they needed. Trade was controlled by the government, which made rules about trading at markets. There were craft workers who made beautiful things, but these were mostly for the *Sapa Inca* and his **nobles.** Craft workers could give the things they made instead of doing **duty work.** This was done by everyone who was not a noble as a kind of tax.

Most craft workers lived and worked in the towns and cities. Those who were the most skilled had workshops in the royal palace. They made things for the *Sapa Inca* and his family. Different parts of the empire were known for people who were skilled in different crafts. The Moche people, for example, produced beautiful pottery, often in the shapes of people or animals. The Paracas people were especially good weavers.

This carefully carved wooden beaker was used during religious ***ceremonies.*** *It shows the head of a noble.*

Weaving

Weaving was one of the most important Inca crafts. The *Sapa Inca* often gave pieces of cloth as presents to **nobles** or to the important people from other groups that were part of the **empire.** Inca women spun their thread so finely and wove it so tightly that the cloth was very good at keeping out the cold. Cloth for a shirt, made on a modern weaving machine, has about 60 **weft** threads in each inch. Ordinary Inca weavers made cloth with 200 weft threads to the inch. The best weavers could fit 500 weft threads into an inch.

This weaving basket is more than 500 years old. The vegetable dyes used on the yarn still have not faded.

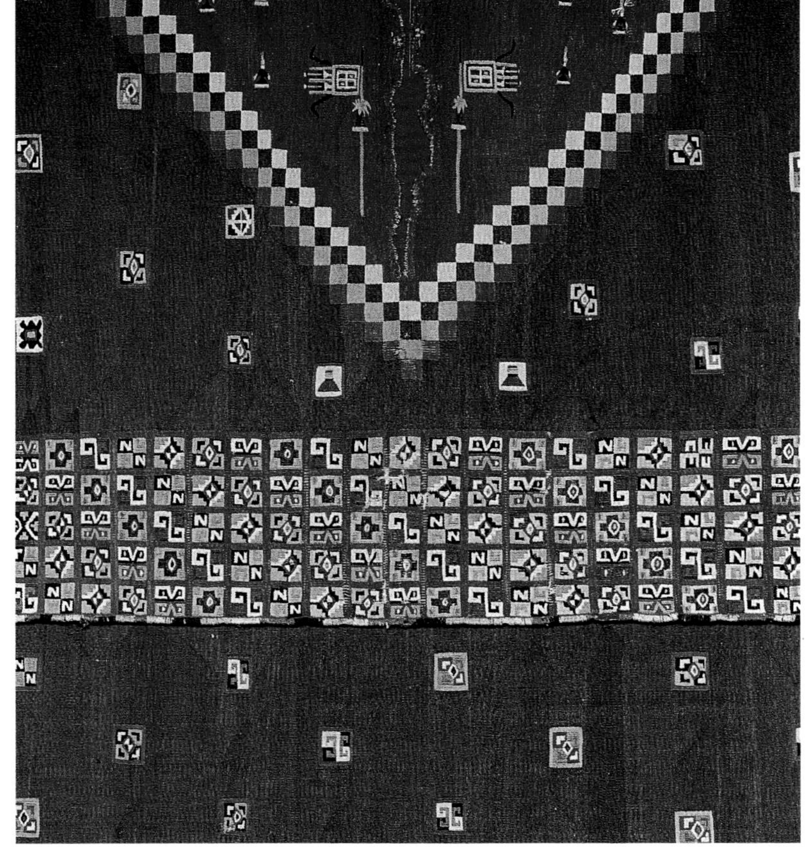

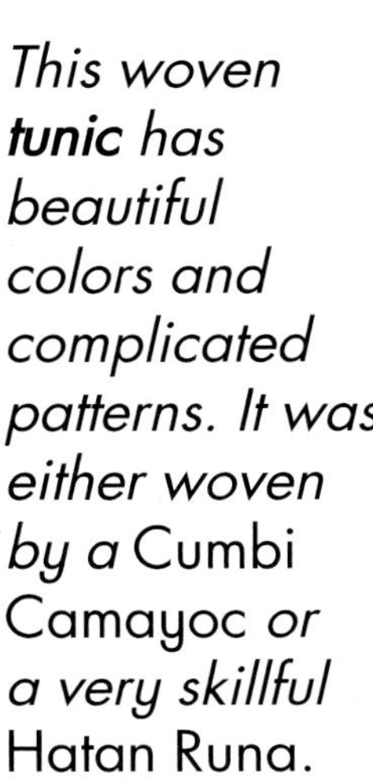

*This woven **tunic** has beautiful colors and complicated patterns. It was either woven by a* Cumbi Camayoc *or a very skillful* Hatan Runa.

The government divided weavers into four groups. There were rules about the kinds of cloth each group could make, and about the colors and decoration they could use.

The first groups were ordinary people who wove their own cloth at home. Weaving was not their only job. The other three groups were all full-time weavers. The *Hatan Runa* did the most basic weaving, such as ordinary clothes. The *Cumbi Camayoc* were more skillful and wove cloth for the **nobles** and for the *Sapa Inca* to give as presents. The most important weavers were the *Mamacuna,* who wove cloth for the **temples** and for the *Sapa Inca.*

Religion

The Incas believed in many different gods and goddesses, who ran most parts of everyday life. These gods and goddesses had to be kept happy with offerings and **sacrifices.** About one-third of every year was taken up with religious **festivals.**

The most important god was Viracocha, who created everything. But the Incas built more **temples** to Inti, the Sun god, than any other god. The Incas believed that prayers and offerings pleased the gods. Sometimes they sacrificed animals, too. They only sacrificed humans if there was a terrible disaster.

This pottery jar has been made to look like a priest sitting down.

The Inca wrapped some of their dead in many layers of cloth. They were wrapped with their knees bent, so they often looked like bundles of cloth. This wooden mask was put on the top of a "mummy bundle," to make a face where the head was.

The Incas worshipped nature as well as gods and goddesses. There were special holy places, often near rivers or mountain tops, where people could go at any time to pray and leave offerings.

The Incas believed in an **afterlife.** They buried their dead with the things they would need after death. People who were good in life went to heaven. People who were bad stayed in this life as invisible **spirits.** These spirits needed offerings or they would bring disaster, just like the more powerful gods and goddesses could. If people did something bad they could make up for it by doing a **penance** given to them by a priest.

Cities

Inca buildings in the cities were made of stone and had high walls with no windows. The streets were paved and narrow. Government officials ran the **empire** from these cities, and priests held religious **ceremonies** at the **temples.** The *Sapa Inca* and his family lived in a palace in Cuzco. Behind the palace was a school where the boys who would one day run the empire were taught how to make and read ***quipu.*** They also learned math, astronomy, history, and mapmaking. The homes and workshops of various craft workers were farther from the city.

The city of Machu Picchu was built on a mountaintop, very close to an even higher mountain. Its location may have given it special religious importance.

You can see how well the stones in this Inca wall fit together and how they curve in where they join.

Cities were built from stone. The blocks were of different colors and sizes, depending on how important the building was. Buildings were not decorated with carvings on the outside. Instead, the stones were carefully smoothed and often curved in to the point where they joined.

Inca builders did not use any **mortar** to fix the stones together. The stones were carved so exactly to shape that they fit perfectly. This method of building meant that in earthquakes, which happened often, the blocks of stone "jumped" and then settled back into place.

Food and Farming

Each year Inca officials measured the farmland and divided it into *tupus.* These were pieces of land of different sizes that produced a certain amount of food. A couple were given one *tupu* and two llamas when they married. They got more land as they had children—one *tupu* for a boy, and half a *tupu* for a girl.

Much of the land was steep, so the Incas farmed by making **terraces.** This gave them thin bands of flat land to farm. They used bird droppings and human waste to keep the soil fertile. In some places they had to bring water to the fields in stone channels to **irrigate** the land.

Farmers in Peru still use terraces, and their methods are very similar to the Incas'. It would be hard to use machines to farm the thin strips of terracing.

Farmers grew corn and a grain called *quinoa,* which grew well high in the mountains. They also grew potatoes, squash, beans, watermelons, peppers, avocados, pears, plums, and cocoa. They grew cotton and kept llamas and alpacas for their wool. They kept dogs and guinea pigs for meat and hunted wild animals. Food was cooked over an open fire. Ordinary people mostly ate bread, porridge, and vegetables.

Corn was the most important crop. It could be made into flat bread, porridge, and beer. There were religious **ceremonies** when the corn was planted. Everyone, even the *Sapa Inca,* planted corn, but the *Sapa Inca* did not work for long.

This statue shows a shaman. A shaman was part priest, part doctor. They used herbs grown by the farmers in their medicines.

Families

All Incas lived and worked in large family groups called ***ayllu.*** All the *ayllu* in a village farmed the land together. In all families, no matter how important they were, men and women did different kinds of work. Men worked outside the home. This work could be running the **empire,** making pots in the city, or farming the land. Women worked in the home. Women from ordinary families took care of the children, cooked, and made cloth and baskets. Women from important families made sure that servants did these jobs properly.

The carvings on this bowl show people going about their daily lives. Men farmed and looked after the animals. Women spun wool, wove, and took care of the home and children.

Children were brought up to do the same work as their parents. Girls learned to run a home and make cloth. Boys learned their fathers' jobs. Boys who were going to be government officials had to go to special schools to learn how to make and read ***quipu.***

Sometimes officials sent ordinary boys they thought were especially clever to these schools. They also chose girls to go to schools that trained the *Mamacuna*—the most skilled weavers. Children had to leave their *ayllu* to go to these schools, but it was a way to move into a more important level of Inca life.

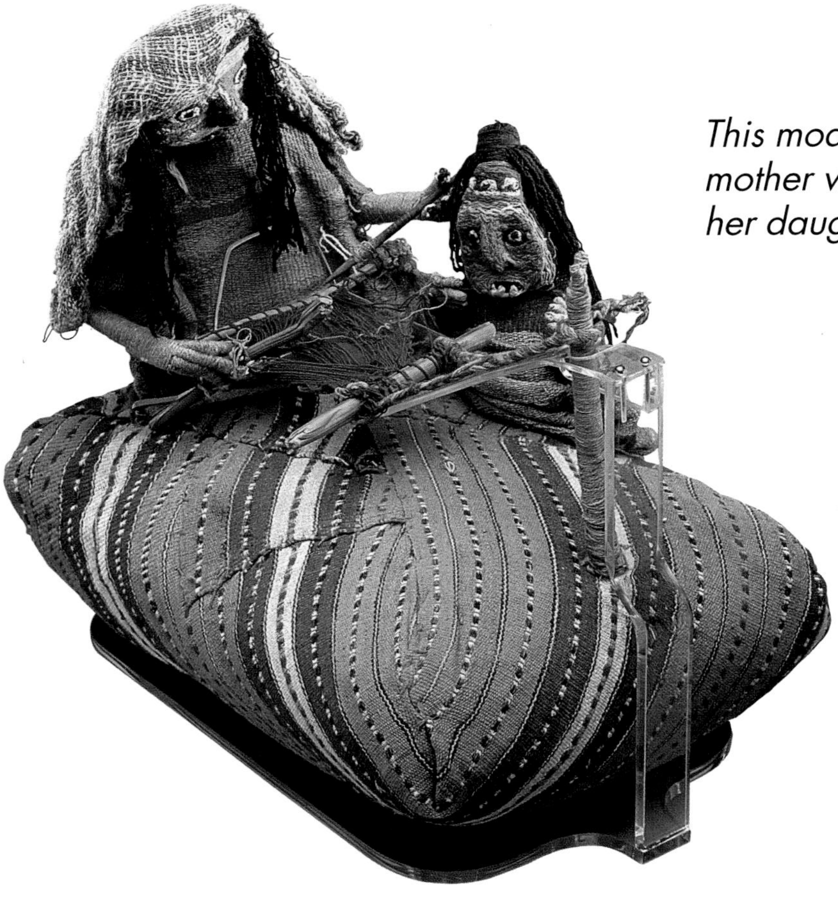

This model shows a mother weaving, with her daughter watching.

Clothes

Most people wore hats made from wool or cotton. They were often knitted, but some were woven.

Most Incas wore a similar style of clothing. The cloth was spun and woven from cotton or wool. It was dyed with plant dyes, which made many different colors. Men wore **loincloths** and **tunics.** The length of the tunic varied, depending on the weather. Women wore long tunics with a belt around the middle, or short tunics with a long skirt. Everyone wore capes tied or pinned together over their other clothes. Sandals were made from woven leaves and wool or animal skins.

The style of clothes was the same for all Incas. However, you could tell how important a person was by how well their cloth was made and how brightly colored and decorated it was. You can work out how important the people in the picture below are by what they are wearing.

Homes

Each ***ayllu*** lived in a set of rooms around a courtyard. People spent most of their time outside. The Incas built their houses from stone or mud bricks on a stone base, with a dirt floor. Roofs were covered in branches, then reeds or grass.

Each room was usually about 13 feet (4 meters) by 5 feet (1.5 meters), with one doorway and no windows. Each room was separate. If a house had two floors, the stairs to the top floor were outside. Ordinary people did not have much furniture, except for a sleeping platform and a few mats. There were places in the wall to store pots and baskets. Clothes were hung on pegs.

Inca homes did not have much furniture, but even ordinary people had beautifully decorated pottery bowls and jars.

Homes had very steep roofs, to carry away the rain.

The way this man is dressed shows he is probably the leader of the ayllu.

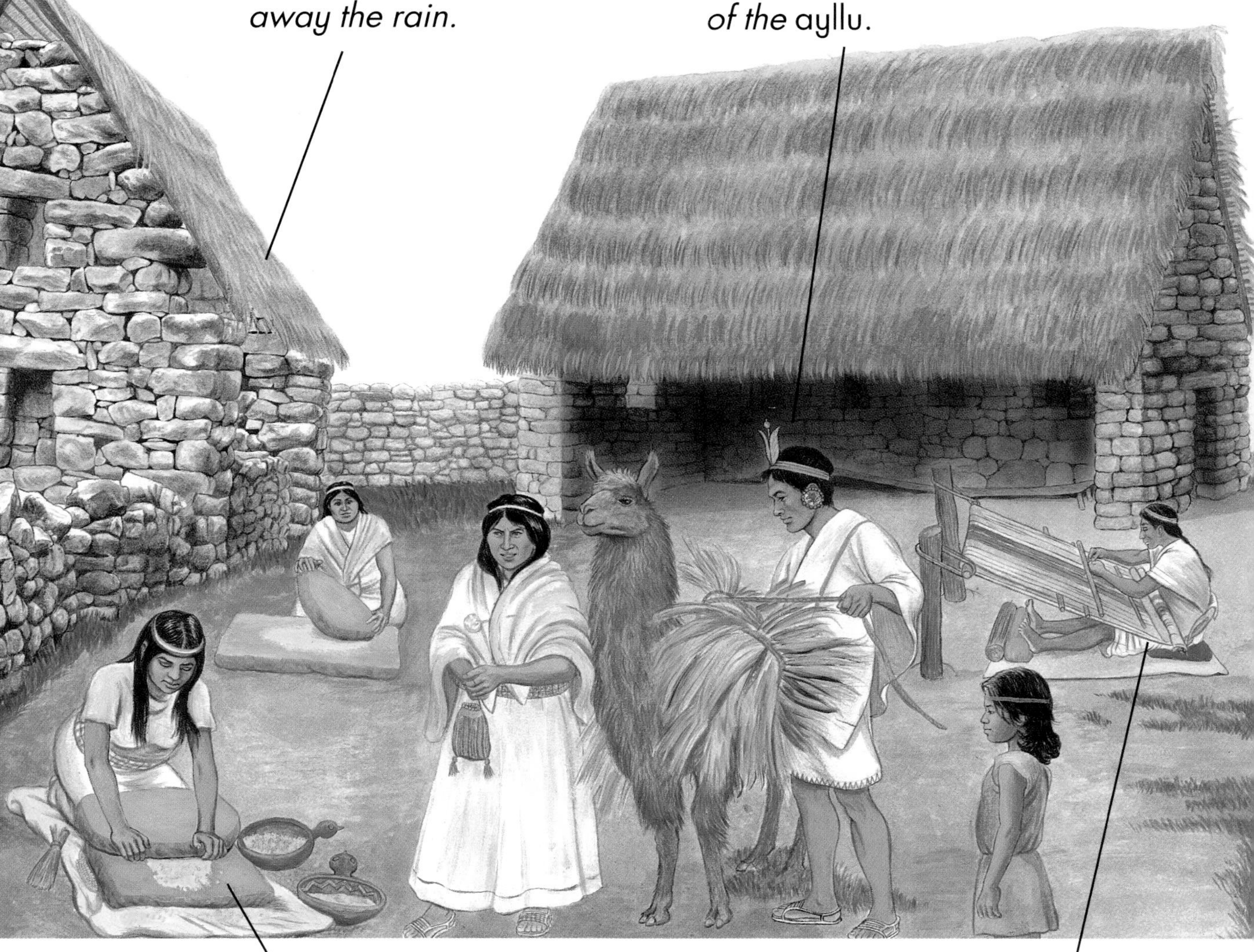

Grinding corn to make bread and porridge took a lot of time.

This woman is using a backstrap loom. She keeps the threads straight by tying them tight behind her back. This was the widest that backstrap looms ever were.

End of Empire

In 1525 the Inca **empire** had stopped growing, but it was running smoothly. But that year a deadly illness swept the empire, killing many people, including the *Sapa Inca.* He had just split the empire between his two sons.

When the Spanish landed at Tumbez in 1532, the empire was split and still weakened by all the deaths from the disease. By 1533 the Spanish had taken over. At first they ruled by using Inca kings who would obey them. But in 1571 they killed the last one of these and put Spanish governors in charge.

The Spanish brought their own beliefs. They did not want the Incas to worship their own gods. In Cuzco they destroyed the Inca ***temple*** *of the Sun and built this Catholic church on top of it.*

Glossary

ayllu organized group of related families

ceremony set of acts that has religious meaning

duty work work that someone must do for their ruler as a sort of tax

empire group of territories or lands controlled by one country

festival time of celebration with special events and entertainment

irrigate to bring water to crops

loincloth short skirt that covers the part of the body between the waist and thighs

mortar material used to stick rocks or bricks together

noble important person of high birth or rank

penance something that is done to make up for having done something bad

quipu group of knotted strings used for keeping records

rebellion rising up against a ruler or government

sacrifice to kill or destroy something as an offering to a god

spirit being that has life but cannot be seen

temple building for religious worship

terrace area of flat land made on a hillside so that it can be farmed

tunic knee-length belted garment

weft in weaving, one of the threads that runs across the loom

More Books to Read

An older reader can help you with these books:

Mann, Elizabeth. *Machu Picchu: The Story of the Amazing Incas & Their City in the Clouds.* New York: Mikaya Press, 2000.

Rees, Rosemary. *The Incas.* Chicago: Heinemann Library, 1999.

Scheff, Duncan. *Incas.* Austin, Tex.: Raintree Steck-Vaughn, 2001.

Pronunciation Guide

ayllu ay-lee-oo
chasqui CHAS-kee
Chimu CHEE-moo
Cumbi Camayoc KUM-bee ka-MY-ock
curaca koo-rah-kah
Cuzco KOOS-koh
Hatan Runa HAT-an ROO-nah
Inti IN-tee
Machu Picchu MAH-choo PEE-choo
Mamacuna MA-ma KOO-na
mitimaes mit-i-mays
Moche MOH-chay
Quechua KETCH-wah
quinoa KEEN-wah
quipu KEE-poo
Sapa Inca SAH-pah IN-kah
Tahuantinsuyu tah-wan-tin-SOO-you
tupu too-poo
Viracocha weer-ah-KOH-chah

Index